# Sense 4 Love

## Empowering Reflections

## About

## Love and Relationships

### G Betancur

# DEDICATION

To one who has endured the pain
Of a broken heart
The sorrow of a forced "Good Bye"
The darkness of a sleepless night

That rock bottom nobody wants to hit

To the one who wants to live
Even when one day
Just wanted to die

To the one who wants to heal
The one who wants to dream
The one who wants to learn
To Love their life again

# What to expect from this book?

*It is tangible tool for a journey of superation and recovery from any emotional setback.*

This book is the written Manual to the journey of the Video Visualization's Collection in the YouTube Channel of the same name which helps to transcend focus at a subconscious level, and absorb Powerful Positive Suggestions and profound affirmations that are given as strong statements with hypnotic visuals over entrancing music. The transformative recovery and success of this unique and entrancing experience will quickly free you from negative obsessive thinking and leads you to cultivate your mind with a much more positive perspective.

The book is packed with inspiring affirmations and supportive profound statements for those going through a difficult period of Heartbreak due to separation, loss, toxic distancing, or a romantic breakup. It of course is a practical manual for those who appreciate the power of affirmations for daily re-energizing, mind nourishment and regular self confidence and inspiration.

This book together with the free YouTube videos, which are a vital part of this healing journey, will revolutionize your life in the way you process your emotions while rewiring your thought pattern for a breakthrough from a difficult emotional and painful situation to find meaning, inner growth, and healing in a fast and rather entertaining way.

The journey begins with a set of life reassuring statements for those experiencing hardship and unhappiness but as the journey progresses, a variety of relationships issues will be referenced and tackled.

Chapter 2, the longest chapter and the only one written in narrative mode, helps with understanding the psychological stages to process a break-up. Bringing awareness of reactions and surrounding beliefs for those who are going through this most common and difficult period; to then continue with powerful inspiring and affirmative statements for mind empowering and liberation. There's also reference to those forced to distance from loved yet toxic and narcissistic relationships on a couple of chapters and related videos.

A few calming guided meditations and powerful affirmations to attract love and a new ideal partner together with hypnotic visualizations, will help you clear your mind, accept any change and continue empowering yourself to open your heart to love again.

The book also includes a collection of abstract artistic images from the hypnotic visuals that relate to the hypnotic visuals on each of the videos.

Give yourself a good break. This program is a mind trip of the best kind.

Enjoy

# TABLE OF CONTENTS

# Preface

There are times in our lives, especially when we go through a period of heartbreak, when we must empower our thinking while processing our emotions and our vision for the future; to help us accept our present situation and progress into something better, rather than let a disappointing situation destroy us.

Sometimes, a lack of perspective could push someone into a spiral of despair and even suicide. It's even awkward to discuss our private reasoning at a time when we hardly trust anyone. It is at these times when we should pay attention to what we are nourishing our minds with. The healthiest thing is not only to try to get out of our head by entertaining ourselves but train our brain's perspective onto a better frame of mind; to process our feelings and be able to embrace a new beginning.

I've been through times such as these and on finding my balance; I created a series of personal statements that helped me immensely. After some editing, they are now made public with this book followed by videos which will be made also public on a YouTube's Channel of the same name.

Most Sense 4 Love's chapters  have now been recorded in videos over hypnotic visuals and entrancing music, it is a powerful program packed with healing content as in conjunction with the hypnotic visuals, will help you to get back at your inner balance and peace.

The time it takes to move on and feel better, changes for different people. But as you can listen to the hypnotic videos as many times as you like and for as long as you need to, they will certainly be a fast and enjoyable way to process your feelings and emotions without anyone imposing timeframes on you.

As I mentioned in one of the videos, it can indeed be a Make or Break situation, and I can assure you, that your future lies as a reflection of your frame of mind and your reactions which, if positively directed, will either turn the situation around or help you to find a new level of self-awareness that will guide you to your true happiness.

English is not my first language; this book clarifies any words you may find hard to understand in any of the videos. You are welcome to join the YouTube channel and hope you find the statements, videos, and surrealistic graphic artwork, valuable and inspiring.

Feel free to share any of the videos and recommend this book to anyone you think may be helpful.

# Life Has a Choice

Life
A journey of periodic cycles
In constant motion and readjustment
Activating our processes of development and inner
growth

The sudden realization that a chapter in our lives is
bound to end
It's usually shocking,
Every time a cycle ends, you undergo a
transformation that might be very painful.
As you, will have to leave parts
Of an old self behind

You may choose to live and embrace
Every new chapter in your life
Trusting, these transformations are necessary
As life continues, the path to your true destiny

Life is giving you a choice
To choose your Happiness over
And walk through this!

You can choose to walk your path rising above the
noise and confusion.
To trust your destiny and be open
To a new experience every day

Your journey and your experiences
Are yours to understand
And no matter what is happening right now,
You should be proud of your story
And who you are

You own every part of your life
And you might be wise to choose
What belongs to it
It is you who must decide
To be honest with yourself
And accept any necessary changes

Letting go of people, places or situations
Is never easy
You must take care of your body, your soul,
your mind.

Your mind is interconnected to the Divine
And you have access to all of its wisdom

Only you can decide to make peace
With all that is happening
In this experience called: "your life"

If you forgive yourself
And those who have ever hurt you
You won't have to carry a nasty tail of
Resentments

You will soar like an eagle

Your heart will be whole to love again
As if never hurt
Embracing what tomorrow brings
Helps you to find true meaning
In the grace of being alive

There would always be new opportunities
On any new day
Choosing to be grateful and honour
The opportunity to experience your life, as it is
Will fill your heart with strength
That force, that comes from deep within you
When you call it

You have been crafted to exist as you are
And after eons of universal preparation
You are now alive
What a magnificent honour!

Your eyes can see the clear sky
You can breathe the fresh oxygen in the air

You are unique
No one can take that away from you.
No matter how much apathy
You may be feeling...
Love lives in you

Your love renews itself as the evergreen grass
Your destiny is yet to be lived
No matter the circumstances.

As you walk in humility and gratitude...
All obstacles are removed from your path
You can surpass all types of challenges each day
And no matter how big or small
Your rewards or lessons will soon show

New rewarding experiences are yet to be lived
You will love and be loved again
You are in constant evolution and understanding

When you radiate pure unconditional
Love and joy
The Universe orchestrates your dreams
And how they manifest into your reality
In perfect time
Whatever you envision for your future, is yours

Even while times are difficult
The line of your story is a masterpiece.
Whatever happens within your story
It's for you to find out its higher purpose
You learn your lessons
From mistakes and fallouts

If you face your truth
And embrace all that is good within you,
You will find a new vision for your future
And gladly, move on
Walking in grace
Full of energy and power
You will be glad to understand that Life
Has all kinds of experiences yet to be lived
Future happy moments worth every effort
To live and strive for

Even if right now life seems to be sour
What is happening to you
Will surely prove beneficial
In one way or another

You can choose to direct all of your thoughts
And actions, to a higher self
And choose the happier way
You can find above chaos

We all go through times of change
What makes the difference
And speeds the process up
Is your reaction to it
And your will to embrace a better future

Life has a choice,
Happiness is a choice.

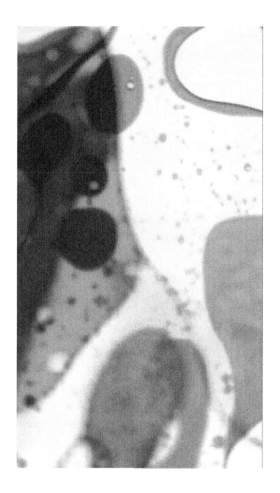

# Your Emotional Stages
# At a Break-Up

When we love someone deeply, we let them enter our very core and allow them to become so much a part of our lives that it is almost unthinkable to be able to continue our normal life without them. Their departure in any shape or form has been compared to the loss of someone through physical death.

Whatever the circumstances and reasons for the breakup, and whoever initiated it, it hurts, so much, as if mourning a death. We have all gone through this at some point in our lives and most adults, even several times throughout life.

This is something you may not want to consider now, but this is the nature of life, ending and beginning processes which are a vital part of our personal inner growth. The saddest thing would actually be never being in love.

Here, we are going to try and rationalize this painful grieving process that has been told to go through stages. Some have numbered the stages of this process as if they would be going in order, however, the stages can happen in any order, as we are all different people and undergo our own way of inner processes according to our psychological needs and expectations

# Denial

At this stage our emotions are going through a roller coaster; we don't seem to be able to accept any logical reason as to why the breakup happened even if there were clear signs that things were not working out or even red flags that things could have gone from bad to worse. We run on our feelings rather than our reason, as if on autopilot. We cannot believe that such a close person is truly leaving! And we find it very hard to adjust to the idea of life without them. We cannot stand what our mind perceives as losing them and all the memories that will go with them! We cling to our memories as our stronghold. Even though we know the relationship is over, we really don't want to believe it, and we are not ready to welcome any advice from anyone around us who tries to make us realize this ending, we can't help but entertain ideas of how we can make things get better and somehow get back at trying to make things work out again. We hold onto any hope, in the clear evidence that it is over.

This is the most dangerous stage where our erratic impulses could get us much worse by constant attempts to contact this person, whatever means we have. Easy tools like text could become a misused weapon that would work against us while refusing to let go and accept the new reality that at this time feels like our worst nightmare.

You have given all the love you think you have to that one person and it makes you feel like your whole world is ending.

This is the most difficult stage to endure; but as if a dark illusion, it will pass. The reactions you have at this stage are crucial as to how deep will you fall or how quickly will you rise.

Sometimes it may indeed be a Make or Break situation, but there is nothing you can do or say to change things at present.

## Escapism

After the initial obvious shock, we may blame ourselves for things going wrong. We look at our memories with a self-critical eye which can be detrimental and could cause great damage to our self-esteem.

It is a volatile time when you may experience intense feelings of regret, guilt, and impulsiveness. You want to stop your fixed thinking about your situation so you seek to distract yourself from this.

Escapism could be positive when you occupy your mind with something productive like work or a new hobby. Unfortunately, the majority of people do a lot of crazy things during this stage. Getting involved too soon in random affairs; one-night stands that lack any bonding and may hurt other people. Drinking and drugs are the most common ways of escape.

As reality kicks in, you want to avoid facing it and desperately try to find some relief. You're running from all your complicated mixture of emotions and you just want to hang on to anything that could keep you numbed out of your emotional turmoil.

This is the stage where you should exercise most care for yourself, as you may be giving into taking action on impulses that you may regret later.

## Anger

Anger can manifest in great disappointment against yourself, the other person, and anybody else that you think could have caused the breakup. If you blame yourself, it could cause you to doubt yourself and go through the other painful stages I will mention later. If you blame the other person for the way you have been let down, it makes you see things differently. Anger if being assertive and controlled is not necessarily a bad thing. If it's not released in any way of aggression, your anger could be used in your favour to help you to move on from the idealistic image which gets you stuck on this person.

You could blame God or the universe which will cause you to feel very discouraged and to lose faith in your future. You might get angry at people or situations associated with the break-up. Anger could get directed at the people that might have been around this person at the time you now perceive they started to change, anger at those who don't seem to understand or agree with your views, and friends who would not take your side and stand for you.

This is the stage where you could also hurt your other relationships and the worst time to engage in any type of communication with your no-longer lover because your passion is being reversed with a very negative force. You may think it's crucial to let this person know about whatever you think and may feel very tempted to initiate aggressive confrontations with them because you don't want them thinking he or she got away with this or that. Arguments that may damage your relationship even further and put your already hurt self through the unnecessary risk of being demoralized further.

As already mentioned, while anger may appear to be an aggressive state, it does not necessarily turn into any aggression at all, and instead, it could be a way to let go of idealizations to regain your power back. You can then be able to rebuild your self-worth and your independence. When channelled internally in the right way. It may even help you to move on and skip all the other painful stages I will continue to describe.

# Bargaining

Bargaining is a stage where you have not quite moved from the denial stage yet. We call "bargaining" any attempt you have at trying to convince this person of any possible way to make the relationship work again. You will be prompted to call them or send long messages and letters where you try to explain yourself to them. You may want to impress them with constant postings on your social media that may be even silly. You only hope for this person to realize your worth at any rate, since you have lost sense of it yourself.

You may try to get a friend or family member to talk to this person on your behalf. You desperately try to find ways to get your relationship back as it was; in any way, you can think of. You may drastically change the way you look which could be inspiring but you may also try to change what is unique in you and pretend to be someone you are not for the sake of this person's attention. You may even compromise on issues that you clearly should not and, generally speaking, adjust your standards into submitting to the idea of this person's opinion on you. Basically, you give all your power away in placing all the blame for the broken relationship onto you and in trying to fix it back, no matter how much effort it is to you.

Unless you honestly realize you need to improve and correct something, lowering your head to please another is not a way to a happy living. You need to understand that this is a temporary trial, a dark and nasty illusion that will last for as long as you continue to mistrust your self-love and altruistic self.

## Depression

The depression stage just like any other stage can manifest in many different forms to different people. You may be unmotivated to continue with your basic routines as you may feel tired all the time and discouraged to continue practicing your hobbies. As opposed to the distraction stage, you avoid contact with friends as you don't enjoy anything social at all. You could not want to do anything but lay in bed. You feel disconnected and in a sense of loss even when you find yourself around people. You may feel on the verge of tears most of the time and could cry out of the blue at the most inappropriate of places or situations. You may experience changes with sleeping either sleeping too much or too little, as well as your appetite when you either eat too little or could do the opposite and start overeating. There's always the risk of giving into drugs or drinking in excess.

Hopelessness, as the most detrimental and debilitating idea, is the thing that makes you feel lost as if love would never be found in your life again. That no one on earth could bring you back into trusting them for you to love them. That nothing would feel fun ever again. Your mind gets fixed into the feelings as of right now and you cannot see any good in your future ahead.

Hopelessness keeps you from moving on, but you must allow yourself to grieve and be compassionate with yourself at this stage with patience. Time will heal all wounds.

Depression could fall to different levels of low for different people and medical advice may be needed.

## Sadness

Rather than a stage, this is the background theme that goes throughout most of the breakup healing process. You may cry at random times when you hear some songs or think of any memories.

You must cry all you want, as your sadness is healed through your tears. You need to express your sadness and feel your hurt; these feelings of sadness will also pass and as physical wounds, your heart will heal with time as well. It is only normal to feel sad as this is a very difficult time for you. The only danger is to dwell in sadness or depression for too long.

You need support at this stage. If you've gotten too overwhelmed or stuck in these lacking feelings, you may need to seek professional help. Breakups could bring to light past hurts and childhood trauma and now might be a great opportunity to discuss them and heal.

You may overemphasize the situation or over-idealized the person you are breaking up with thinking he/she is the only person you could ever love or could ever love you. You may get wrong ideas about yourself and question whether you're good enough or if even lovable, but once you move from here you won't hurt like this ever again.

## Acceptance

This is the final stage no matter in what order you have now processed the other stages. As if a rainbow after a dark storm, here we see the light and colours of day again and acknowledge the situation for what it is, making peace with ourselves and the other person, whether they know it or not, as we come to terms with our new life and can have a much different perspective than before. We finally see ourselves in the future and can envision single life without the fear of not being in love ever again. This is the time in which we can direct our energy and passion to new interests, whether in work or hobbies or social going on. It doesn't happen all of a sudden, but gradually we start thinking less and less into trying to figure out the other person and the situation, you start to focus on yourself bit by bit as you can start envisioning your future in a more positive light while gaining clarity about what you would like to experience next in your life.

Acceptance doesn't always mean we are happy with the ending of the relationship, though sometimes it does, acceptance is making peace in our minds with ourselves, with our world, and we can now start letting go of the relationship to slowly step forward with our lives. If you feel like this stage will never come, it means you're still struggling within any of the previous stages. Rest assured this time will come. This whole breakup situation is nothing but a cycle in life. This is a time where you will feel proud of having overcome all the other stages and would bring an immense sense of meaning to your life.

We cannot put a time frame into how long any stage would last. Different people take different speeds at how they process their emotions, but regardless of how long it takes, it will get here for sure.

One thing to understand about this healing process is that these stages are not defined rules. The stages may be experienced in a different order. Some stages can relapse more than once and one stage or various stages could skip entirely.

However long these stages take, it helps a great deal to identify them so you can understand where you are at and treat yourself with care, to apply any necessary restrain to harmful impulses, to grieve for as long as you need to cope with your emotions and to also apply patience and honesty to allow your progress into full true acceptance.

One day you will realize you have truly moved on and this is a day worth striving for.

The day comes when you will not even think about your past relationship anymore and can connect with a new love if and when that happens. When your future self is happy in a new situation, which in general, feels much better for you, you'll be grateful that this past relationship didn't work out, and in fact, you may not even think of it at all!

# Reason Season Lesson

Every person comes into your life
For a reason, a season, or a lesson

A reason
To push you into necessary changes
A season
To live a new experience for a time
A lesson
To understand what you really want in life
And know yourself better

All being an intrinsic part
Of your personal growth
Not all romantic relationships are meant to stay
You must give them the freedom
To choose their purpose
And love yourself enough
To embrace what is true

Relationships never end
We are all in this together; as long as we live.
We are all in each other's lives
Whether we realize it or not
Relationships can evolve
Or transform into something new

We are each other's chapters
In all of our life stories
Every life story is an ethereal book
That won't ever be erased; neither rewritten

When we pass a page
It is best to leave a good record behind

When someone passes their page on us
It's best to leave them with a good memory
And let them go in peace
If something went wrong
The grace of forgiveness is available to all

Everything happens at a moment in time
Is human nature to feel regrets
But dwelling on faults of the past
Does not benefit anyone

We can forgive ourselves
And be able to forgive others.
Whether they care to know it or not

Others may choose to forgive us
But if they don't
That should no longer be our burden.

We must kindly state our truth and say
All we need to say in time.
As unsaid words
Can keep us chained for a long time

An apology, an "I love you", a "Goodbye"

We can only do our best
But if that is not possible at present
We must find that closure within ourselves

Truth will take care of itself
Love sometimes needs to be tested
To be able to evolve into something better

If you let it go free
It may come back to be yours forever
If it doesn't
It never was

Just rest assured it is for the best
As clinging from a tread of lack of love
Can only make you forever suffer

Love is solid and free
Love is eternal
And will manifest
In many forms throughout our lives
Love will breathe in and out
New characters in your story

As you continue to learn

Its Reasons Seasons and Lessons

# When You Stand for Yourself

When you stand for yourself

You chose to live this new experience with all the
courage it requires

Your recovery from pain to happiness is your
priority
You refuse to dwell in images in your mind
that cause you sadness
You refuse to think of people and situations
that make you sad
You decide to dream instead and imagine a
beautiful outcome regardless of what others
think
Only you know the way you feel
You can control your emotions
You see the possibilities to bring balance
At this moment you don't urge for anything
neither reject anything
You simply take a pause to breathe and feel
All will be as it will be and there is nothing
you need to do to change it
You do cry if you feel like it and let my
emotions run like a river for a time
You then, take a pause to stand again
The situation can change on its own if it will
As there is no need to force anything
You relax in the trust you have in true love
and the universe

That all that is happening, is for the benefit of
all involved
You can relax, you command yourself to relax
and so you do
You can wait for the unfolding of the plan
that the universe has for you
You envision happiness, joy, and love as
blessings coming your way
Whatever is happening in your life, it will be
resolved
You relax in the trust you have in true love
and the universe
That all that is happening, is for the benefit of
all involved
You can relax, you command yourself to relax
and so you do
You can wait for the unfolding of the plan
that the universe has for you
You envision happiness, joy, and love as
blessings coming your way
Whatever is happening in your life, it will be
resolved
There is no problem without a solution
There may be great things you don't
understand right now
But you can be sure that Love has your back
Love is the force that moves the universe, you
can trust Love
Love nurtures and protects
There are blessings that require divine timing
to come forward
And you can be patient; patience turns into
excitement to receive the new

Your peace will ensure the process you must
go through goes faster
You simply rest your mind in trusting Love as
a rock.
True Love is the most powerful force in the
universe
If a relationship does not hold enough love,
you attract one that will do
When you stand for yourself
You take care of yourself
You embrace every day in your precious life
To be open to experience something
NEW

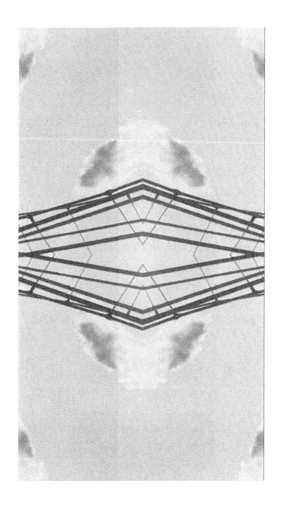

# Confident

Be confident
That the forces in the universe
Are on your side

And that being happier every day is your choice

You are the leading character in your story
And you must value yourself immensely

You have the power to share your love
With whomever you choose to.
You also have the power to reserve that love.
And focus on your wellbeing

No one can take away from you
The will to live and love

Love is always and forever be renewed
In the many different experiences
You are due to live.

You can decide to abandon
Any obsessive desire in your mind

To appreciate those who love you
For as long as they stay

And to ignore those who don't

You have the grace to forgive
And the power to stand up
To truly loving yourself and your life

Ditching away any resentment
That stops true love from flowing freely

You can embrace your future's vision
As a new challenge
To open your heart to love
To changes in life
And to be positive

Only you can decide
To fill your heart with love
And your mind with peace

You will be grateful
For all that you've lived

Every person and circumstance
Is a unique part of your development
And your story

You can ask for strength
And feel the forces
Summoned up at work within yourself

You are never alone
When you ask, you shall receive

You will be filled with courage

To embrace a new path
To hold your chin up and free yourself
From regrets of the past

Your life is meant to be lived with passion
You can rest assured that you can succeed
In whatever you focus your passion on

You will forever be intertwined with love
That same force that brought you to be Alive

You deserve to experience the life you've chosen
To its fullest
New experiences are now on your way

You must clear your mind
So it can produce new ideas.
To embrace Life and
The Love you can find every day in Nature
Nature is a pure source of energy

Your mind understands your answers
When it taps into infinite intelligence
This intelligence is open to all of us
And will reveal its guidance to you in due time
You will be clearly guided in a time of need.
To conquer whatever challenge comes your way

You must detach
From toxic people and toxic situations
Peacefully leave them all behind
You must continue to grow and evolve
To experience the story of your life

As best you can.

Life will always bring something new...
To appreciate... and to experience

You can refuse to think of anyone or anything
That makes you sad
You will start a new loving and peaceful chapter
When you are ready to

Let a rain of peace wash away your worries
Trust that the forces
That gave you life in this universe
Got your back

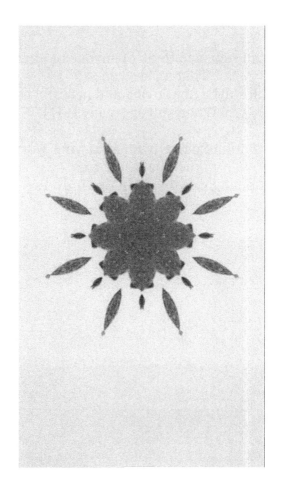

# Attracting Love

The love you want easily finds you
The love you want
It's wanting you
You are lovely
You are lovable
You are loving
You are love
You attract true love
You are open to receive and to give love
Your inner peace dissolves
Any barrier to true love
Your inner joy dissolves any fear
You are free to love again
Any block between you
And true unconditional love
Is vanishing now
Your heart is clear
Your mind is at peace
Your life is whole
You don't need to chase
You receive
Love is looking for you
Your door is open to true love
The love you want, it's wanting you
You are lovely
You are lovable
You are loving
You are love

You attract true love
The love you want
Is wanting you
The love you want easily finds you
You are lovely
You are lovable
You are loving
You are love
You attract true love
You are open to receive and to give love
Your inner peace dissolves
Any barrier to true love
Your inner joy dissolves any fear
You are free from chains of the past
You are free to love again
Any block between you
And true unconditional love
It's vanishing now.
Your heart is clear
Your mind is at peace
Your life is whole
You don't need to chase
You receive
Love is looking for you

The love you want easily finds you
Your door is open to true love.

# Mindful Shower

Welcome

This mind shower of induced affirmations
And visualizations will positively reprogram
Your subconscious mind

Allow your mind to be open an
Let your usual thoughts drift by
Without paying any attention to them
Just for now
Be aware of your breathing
In deeply and out slowly

And as you continue breathing
Synch in as to follow your inner flow
Feel your lungs receiving the oxygen in the air.

Enjoy yourself while being calm
As you let all tension melt away.
Observe how light your body feels.
You can now use your imagination
To draw into your life, anything you like
.

Visualize yourself smiling from the inside,
Feeling the invisible breeze
That softly caresses your bare skin
Your face

You feel safe

You feel connected
To that universal loving energy
That has always taken care of you

You deep down know that you can succeed
At whatever your heart truly desires

When you trust, you easily, let go
When you let go of any control
You can relax on this knowing
You win at this game called life
The universe wants you to win
Every single time

You are deeply loved

Your story is a precious valuable record
In the story of life itself

Remember yourself as a child
Laughing, having fun, and feeling good
Relax your face
Let calmness saturate your mind.

You are a human being,
With strengths and weaknesses
In constant evolution
Your life story is unique
In the whole of the universe
You are loved,

As you are willing to evolve and grow
You are peaceful

You are courageous
You have always been
Since the day you'd chosen to be born.
You do your best to be a better person each day.

Whatever you go through in life
Makes you stronger, wiser, and more interesting
You are strong enough to fight any battle

You understand human nature
You are compassionate yet don't allow
Other people's behaviours and opinions
To take any control over you

You enjoy your life experiences
And help others when you can.
You take care of your needs and
Support your personal decisions.
Your intuition directs you
To succeed time and time again

You surpass any obstacle
The universe as your higher self
Is always by your side

You take care of yourself
You eat healthily, you sleep long enough.
You have a sound and assertive mind
You can discern people and their intentions.
You are a great judge of character

You are an active achiever

You have loads of energy to execute your work
You allow positive thoughts into your mind
You are willing to continue learning

You have so much energy
That exercising is a joy
You treat everyone with kindness
You smile at people often.

Life is a gift. Life is a miracle
Life is a great adventure around the sun
You forgive the faults and failures
Of people concerning you
Deep down everyone
Is trying their best
Just like you.

You are destined to achieve your goals
When you don't give up on them

You came into this world
To be Successful and Happy

# Moving On

You are moving on
You are no longer dwelling
On those who hurt you.
You are compassionate
For all the pain you have exposed yourself to

You are now taking care of your mind
Your heart, your soul
You are no longer attached to the pain
That others inflict on you
You are walking away from people and situations
that make you suffer

You are in control of your mind
And all of your thoughts
You are walking away from suffering
You are intelligent and wise
You are in total control of your emotions
You are serene yet powerful
You are free to decide on your future

You are making better choices
To connect with others
You are strong and at peace
With any changes in your life
You are moving on
You are walking ahead to find your true destiny.
You are trying to be a better person every day.
You are unique and beautiful
In your very own special way
You have been crafted the way that you are

You acknowledge your flaws
You do your best to improve
You value yourself for all that you are
Your life story has not finished yet
It is not over until it's over

You do care for your health and your well-being
You are free, as you remove the chains
That bound you to the past.
You are a free spirit
You choose to embrace what is good in your life.
You are full of courage
And you face your reality as it is.

You are determined to make any necessary changes
to the way you think, live, and love.

You are a human being
Experiencing natural growth
You are reaching out for your true purpose
You have the inner power
To stand on your decisions
You are grateful for your progress

Your life is always changing
This is what brings meaning "to be alive"
You accept your present situation

Keep walking
You are willing to learn
You are willing to grow

You are thankful to realize

How much you have already moved on.
You are resolute to live the past in the past.
You are leaving toxic relationships behind
You are leaving toxic situations behind
Where they belong

You are peaceful and loving
You are humble enough
To forgive and to accept any loss
You are now walking towards the new and
It fills you with joy.
You believe in yourself and
In a better vision for your future

You decide to be altruistic and stay calm
You decide to no longer be attached
To any worries in your mind.
To believe in your future

You are a part of everything
And everything is connected to you.
You are inspired to continue
With your life and your story
Setbacks truly made you stronger and wiser

You possess the grace of love
As if you have never been hurt

You are moving on
Your love moves on with you.

# Your New Love

Your next love joins your life when you are ready.
We are now connecting with the infinite possibilities
found within this universe for a list of qualities and
ideas that through visualizations will activate your
subconscious mind to attract
A specific someone who has a load of love to give
and the universe is getting him or her ready for you.

It is someone who awakens your dreams
And helps you to open up your fun self again
You feel great around this person
This is someone to whom you connect
Not just physically but also mentally
In a very healthy way
You can talk about anything at all
You will have great conversations.
It is someone who has a very wide and wise
Appreciation of life
He or She needs nothing from you.
They have everything! But you!
You suddenly feel love again

This is someone who knows
What he or she wants in life
You are the one they are looking for
Honest, loyal, truthful, and genuine.
Who expresses affection freely
Full of purpose and serious yet fun to be with

Someone, whose ambitions are not just financial,

But also personal,
Who strives for a loving future, with you
Is someone you can trust
Who can keep their word
And own their decisions
Who shows you love through actions
More than words

This is someone wise
Who understands what is what
A true real deal

He or she loves who you are
And cares deeply about you
This is someone with a strong character
Kind and tender when relating to you

Emotionally available and open to commit to you
This person is happy just to be with you
He or she enjoys all types of music
But can appreciate silence too
The more they get to know you
The more they love you

Someone whose vitality is contagious
And brings the best out of you
Independent and in positive control of their life
Just as you will be on yours

Is someone generous not only with money
But also with their time and affection
The more you get to know this person
The more you open to love him or her

This is someone who knows
How to get cozy and relax when at home

Who appreciates nature and likes to eat healthily
A very spontaneous person
Who enjoys the simple things
That makes life beautiful and fun
As well as exploring new places

Is someone solid and self-assured
Who is serious to commit, to you!
He or she knows how to deal
With diverse types of people
But more importantly
Knows how to deal with you
Supportive of you and your dreams

This is someone you find
Utterly sexy and a great kisser
Yes, very good looking, for sure, to you!

You suddenly
Love all about the way they carry themselves.
The way they walk, the way they talk
And how they manage to make you love again!
You both respect
And admire each other very much
This is someone who finds the best hangouts
To go with you
And is often up to just having a good time
Making you feel sexy and having fun

Your backgrounds complement each other's

Outlook on life

This is someone worth
All the experience you now have.
You will understand why all other relationships
Failed previously

You'll love him or her
More than you ever loved anyone before.
He or she will love you and respect you
More than anyone has done before

How READY are you to meet this person?
Well...Get ready...

Because you will!

# Sleeping

As you lay down to sleep
You set my mind to rest
Be grateful to have lived another day
Every single day you heal more and more

Get yourself the most comfortable now
And Let all the weight of your care
Sink into your bed
Knowing the universe supports you
Let worrying thoughts drift by and
Ignore what they say right now
Just stop giving any attention to them tonight
There is nothing you must do right now
So just pause your thinking until tomorrow
And wonder how many stars
Are shining in the sky
Your subconscious mind is connected
With the infinite intelligence
That knows all the solutions
To all of your problems

While you sleep
Your mind will find those solutions.
That you will use tomorrow
While you sleep
Your subconscious mind will encounter
The clarity you need for tomorrow
If you rest well
Tomorrow your awakened consciousness
Will reveal the answers you won't find right now

Relax in the infinite support that sustains the earth
gravitating on space,
And all birds and animals at night to be awakened in
the morning
The same supporting force
That has always supported you
Love, the greatest force in the universe
You can trust Love
You have been brought into existence
By this same Love.
You are loved, the universe supports you
Let this love cocoon you into sleeping
Tomorrow is a new day
And as you live your best, one day at a time
Each day will bring you
Progress, solutions, and answers
A peaceful night re-energizes your tomorrow
Love will take care of every single thing
You don't have to do anything at all
Right now, silence and peace will clear vibrations
And attract positive outcomes
For now, you get your mind to rest
You will have time to think again tomorrow,
Love will take care of every single thing
You don't have to do anything at all
You don't have to force anything at all
Your mind is going to rest
As you allow your mind to rest
You allow your body to sleep
Sleep well
Sleep...Sleep

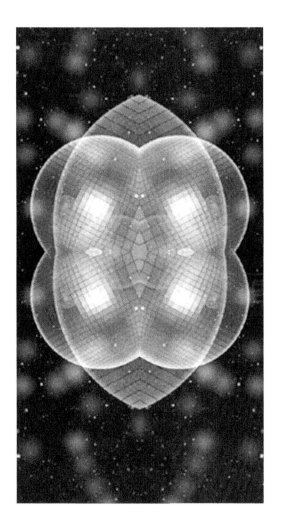

# So Here We Are

So here we are
Full of beautiful memories and an aching heart
You didn't see this coming
It's totally normal to feel sad

The shock is a mixture of desire and regret
The words of others are meaningless
For your busy mind
You feel no one can understand your sorrow
The pain is just too much to endure

In fact, to us, it is a death
Death of a love story we don't finish to complete

The broken dreams
Those are now more precious than ever
That love you gave must come back
To shine again through to you
To love yourself above any situation
To love your future
That is filled with new memories to be made

The love of that someone you haven't met yet

The love for that someone
Who needs their freedom right now
And may return again for the best to come
The love in the universe that
Will always guide you and be there for you.
You must stop the negative scenarios

That plagues your mind right now
You must ignore the loud voices in your head
You must take a deep breath
And jump into the pool of the unknown.
Trusting that there is a force in the universe

That force is love
That force is in you
You can trust yourself
You can trust love

Let your worries fly away with the wind

Start practicing affirmations and meditations
To train yourself for your inner battle

Only you can conquer your own fate

Only you can decide
What thoughts go into your mind
This is just a new chapter in your life
And however difficult
It can change to something better

Take a leap of faith
The only way you win is by getting up
May these words inspire you to take courage
It really is not the end of anybody's world
But a continuation of a great story

Your story

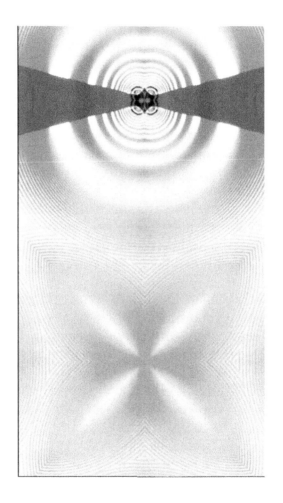

# Love is Joy

When you are in love
You are not supposed to feel pain for long
When You Are in Love
You are supposed to feel joy
Love without joy is not love, not anymore
If love causes you pain, it is now something else that
needs some fixing.

True love makes amends as it goes along
True love will soothe any pain
True love will leave the pain behind
True love fills you with joy
New or Renewed love will wash away the pain
New or Renewed love will make joy
Shine like never before.

After the storm a bright fresh rainbow
Shines through the horizon
New or renewed love
Does not always have to be romantic
Though most times it is
But any kind of love will always bring you joy
The new or renewed love
Reconnecting with family
The new or renewed love
In some friendships
The love of someone new
The deep love within you for your own self

Love heals the pain
Feel the joy this new or renewed love gives you
Joy!! Is just around the corner of your eyes
The giggles
The excitement
The laughter
The fun
Those warm feelings inside
When you are together
The sweet expectation of a beautiful surprise
The flow smiles
The kind gestures
The sweetness in their voice

The melody in someone else's name
Or in a new name
That someone who makes your heart beat faster
The excitement to see them
The beat that makes you move
And sing and dance
The enthusiasm
That makes you jump out of bed every morning
The idyllic fusion of new dreams
That brings you to bed every night

That is joy
That is Love

Love is joy

# Love magnet

As a clear vessel, you are to be filled with love.

You are attracting energy is powerful

Your life story is unique

Your love story is very interesting

Your deeper understanding
Of life and human nature

Makes you very special

You are a magnet to the love
That is looking out there for you
.
You are a love magnet

Someone out there is looking
For exactly someone like you
Someone out there who is
Exactly the one you are looking for

You are attracting each other
At this very moment

The forces in the universe
Are conspiring for this to happen
You are blessed by knowing this

Sometimes something has to end
For something new to emerge

Life transformative energies push you to grow
The struggle between spirit and matter is endless

You must try to center yourself
And find your balance.
The universe will reward your courage
And just like a magnet
You attract all you desire.

You can trust that love is guiding you
To where you belong
You are a magnet
To the love that is looking out here for you.

You are a love magnet

Someone out there is looking for exactly
Someone like you
You are attracting each other
At this very moment
The forces in the universe
Are conspiring for this to happen

You are blessed just by knowing this

You are a love magnet

# Mind a wish

The following exercise can be done either by lying still, closing your eyes if you wish, as well as sitting in a quiet and peaceful place such as a park or a walking path where you are not exposed to any danger relating to traffic or any hazards that you need to be alert for.
You should not be operating any machinery or driving.

This is visualization for people familiar with meditation who understand the process of self-relaxation and breathing awareness to be able to relax and be aware of your breathing throughout its duration.

Begin by being aware of your presence and the rhythm of your breathing. Quiet your mind and relax your physical body from head to toe by imagining a wave of light breaking through any tension and any stiffness from your neck all down through your spine, your legs, and your feet.
Let this light breeze in and out of your head as if clearing out thoughts that take you away from your present moment. You can now command your whole self to relax and so you do...

You are getting ready to visualize time travelling to your fourth dimension.
You are ready to attract

You feel strong, healthy
Vital
Full of energy
Within your body and your mind
You visualize a wonderful walk through a path
Among grown-up green grass and little wild and colourful flowers....
Little wildflowers of many types and colours
Randomly grow within the grass and it is a gorgeous sight.
To those who seldom walk by, like you are doing now...

At some point along the end of this path
You find yourself in front of this big and spacious entrance.
This huge open door leads you to an unfurnished white room of high ceilings, a set of 4 huge windows on each side of its white walls, and marble floors with only a couple of shining chandeliers that hang from its high ceilings.
Soft rays of sunshine get through the windows that overlook the full view of that dreamy garden you just crossed to get to this wonderful place.

It's a beautiful morning, the space looks bright and spacious and you are glowing with excitement as you don't know yet, why you are here but know there must be a good reason.
You see yourself wearing white linen clothes, sandals, and a wide smile on your face.
The fragrance of your favourite perfume fills the place and you are feeling so fresh.

On the other side, there is a next huge opened door that leads you to another room, and as you walk through you find yourself in front of this immense catalogue with pages that double your height, you can actually pass the pages and it looks as if it contains a variety of anything you can think of. This book contains absolutely anything you want to imagine...every single thing.

You just think of something and it appears on the next page. It is an order book, and you can order anything you want....

What would you like to order?

What captivates your eyes?

If there is anything specific that you want, you are able to get it at your wish.

You can make 3 of your orders now....and they will be delivered to you.

Make your orders now


Good, your orders will be delivered to you shortly

You don't have to be concerned about them any longer.

You are here to relax and enjoy the magic of your own mind.

To enjoy this time and trust your deliveries will for sure, get to you in due course

You just relax

You now walk back to the beautiful garden and take a new path through green and leafy trees.

You are allowed to pick the most beautiful flowers along your way, which ones do you see? Which ones do you smell? Which ones do you pick?
The sun shines through the trees and the bird songs accompany you on your way back.
You have nothing to worry about
Nothing stays behind; you deserve to get anything you genuinely want.

You will keep this understanding within your daily thoughts
That you can create beautiful experiences for yourself
To craft your future at your will
To design your scenes for your future as you please

You are determined to defeat any negativity that crosses your way to get to this.
Before you open your eyes, you remind yourself
That, you will keep all the best and most positive thoughts about you and your life
How amazing it all can be now with your orders getting to you.
You appreciate life as a fantastic adventure where anything is possible.
You are blessed with this knowledge, and you are powerful without measure.
When you are blessed you feel humble and so very grateful.
You should do this visualization exercise once a week, just as you do your shopping every week.
You are free to create and change your style and preferences as you want.

And you will for sure be astonished at the results.

As you are now getting back to the present moment,
A sense of joy and expectation fills you
And as you arrive you get ready to wake up.
You are increasingly excited as you expect good deliveries.
In real-time soon!
You are now excited to get up to activate your creative energy.
And at the count of 5

You will just open your eyes and go to enjoy your day.
1 2 3 4 5

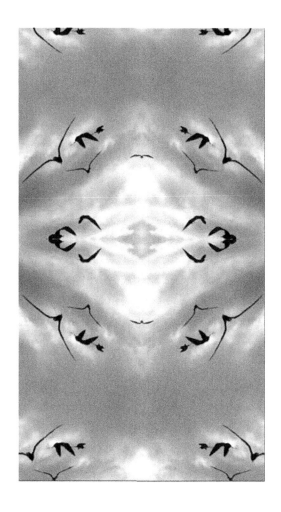

# Grateful

Being grateful
Is more than appreciating something you receive
Being grateful is appreciating all that your very life
has granted you

The automatic work done within your body
To survive and thrive every single day

The sunshine that brings growth
To all those fruits you will consume
The perfect coordination of physics
To keep us afloat in space
The unseen giver of life
To all animals and other humans
Who have a share of this journey

The beautiful planet
With all its astonishing panoramics

The oxygen in the air, we can breathe
And in the water, we can drink
Gratitude to witness another Dusk and Dawn

To be able to feel
To be able to forgive
To be able to Love and Love again
Gratitude is recognizing
That being alive and healthy
Is enough to enjoy the experience
The experience to see, to hear, to talk, to walk

To have this human body
This wonderful work of love and life
To experience the grace to live

Being grateful is to get up when we fall
Because we know it is all part of our learning

Grateful to experience a new chapter
To discover something new
To meet someone new
To believe that love is in charge
That love always wants to be expressed in us

Love fills a grateful heart
A grateful heart is open anew to love
Time and time again

Be grateful for those who love you along the way
For as long as they stay

Those who love you
No matter how many or how few
Are so very precious

There are still many happy moments
To be grateful for

To experience Gratitude
Over and over again

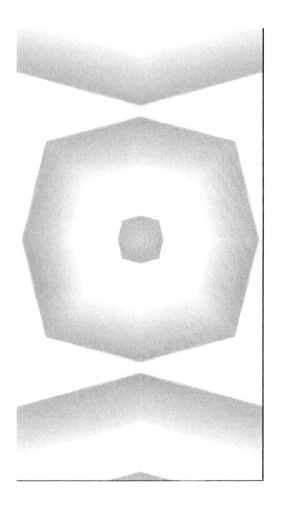

# Dream Walking

The following exercise can be done either by lying still, closing your eyes if you wish, as well as sitting in a quiet and peaceful place such as a park or a walking path where you are not exposed to any danger relating to traffic or any hazards that you need to be alert for.
You should not be operating any machinery or driving.

This is a visualization for people familiar with meditation who understand the process of self-relaxation and breathing awareness to be able to relax and be aware of your breathing throughout its duration.

Begin by being aware of your presence and the rhythm of your breathing. Quiet your mind and relax your physical body from head to toe by imagining a wave of light breaking through any tension and any stiffness from your neck all down through your spine, your legs, and your feet.
Let this light breeze in and out of your head as if clearing out thoughts that take you away from your present moment. You can now command your whole self to relax and so you do...

You are getting ready to visualize time travelling to your fourth dimension.
You are ready to attract.

You feel strong, healthy, vital, full of energy within your body and your mind.

You visualize a wonderful walk through a path among grown-up green grass and little wild and colourful flowers....

The sunshine through the green trees lets you know it is now the afternoon and you are about to meet someone.

Whoever you meet, is someone who brings immense joy to your heart

Whether you know who this person is yet or not, you meet them at a bench at the end of the path among the flowers.

You both greet each other feeling so happy and keep on walking, holding hands tenderly.

You both can't stop smiling as you both get lost in each other's eyes.

The sun is slowly setting as you draw near the beach.

You both take your sandals off to take a barefoot stroll by the shore watching the gorgeous sunset.

Let your emotions be immersed to enjoy this happy and sexy moment

The soft embrace

The peace

The joy

The love

Feeling the caressing sand and the soft water kisses on your feet, you both keep a slow pace.

You have nothing to worry about right now.

You both stop to immerse in a long embrace. You keep watching the orange sunset.

How lovely it feels to lay your head on their body as if listening to their heartbeat.

Feeling this warmth and affection gives you immense peace.
Sweet loving feelings surround your bodies.

Love fills your mind
As you both sit by the sea, a seagull brings you a note, you are asked to make a wish.

The note says, your wish will be granted if the universe considers it is for the benefit of all involved...
Make your wish now

Good, your wish will be granted
You don't have to be concerned about it any longer.
You are here to relax and enjoy the magic of your own mind.
To enjoy this time and trust your wish will for sure get to you in due course.

You just relax

You are now both driving back along the beautiful coast overlooking the ocean.
Feel how cool the wind blows gently upon your hair
You are loved, you are free, you are healthy, you are happy.
You appreciate Love in your life and are deeply grateful to be you and to meet this person.
You have nothing to worry about
Nothing stays behind; you deserve the true love you genuinely want.

You are determined to defeat any negativity that crosses your way to get to this.
Before you open your eyes, you remind yourself
That, you will keep all the best and most positive thoughts about you and your life
And how amazing it all can be now that your wish will come true!
You appreciate life as a fantastic adventure where anything is possible
When you are blessed you feel humble and so very grateful
As you are now getting back at the present moment
A sense of joy and expectation fills you

As you arrive you get ready to wake up
You are increasingly excited
As you expect your wish to come true in real-time soon!
You are now excited to get up and to activate your creative energy
And at the count of 5
You will just open your eyes and go to enjoy your day. 1.2.3.4.5.

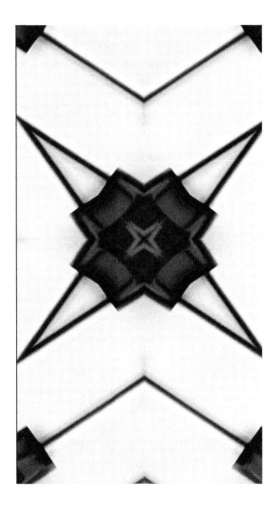

# You now Know

You now know what is what

You can now connect the dots
They can no longer fool you
You know what Love feels like
You know what love is like
You know what you do when you love someone

You know what is love
And you know what is not
No one can cover the sun with one of their fingers
anymore

Yes you deserve to be loved
You are open to crossing that gate
That takes you on a new journey
An inner discovery of your true nature
You can now choose your true tribe
Not everyone in the past belongs to it

You are now open to true love
You are ready to walk your walk
You are strong to stay alone for as long as it takes
To have the patience
To develop within the process
To have faith to envision a truly happy future

You deserve to be loved
You will only give your love to those who deserve it
It is normal to feel unwanted emotions

This awful time will pass
No one has the power
To make you bitter or unlovable
Your true nature is that of love
You are now ready
To ditch all those people or memories
That fooled you onto something else
The ones that attempted
To make you lose your mind
Your self-esteem and your values
You no longer play into
Their mind games and narcissistic antics

You deserve true love
You now know what is real
You are now willing and open
To experiencing true love and love in abundance
You can love again and be loved as you deserve
You have not wasted any time

Life is supposed to teach you lessons
You now know what is what
You are now ready to experience true love
You now know better
You now know best
You now know what is what.

# No One Like You

Don't ever wonder
What a traitor's fate would be like?
It may even be fun and empowering for them
For a while
But soon their ego feast is over
Fireplaces and full moons
Will always remind them of you
There's no one like you

You gave that person your true love
The kind of love that others search a lifetime for
The kind of love other's have died for
Yet they chose to rather walk away
Than strive for it to survive
Among some few evil tongues

They may walk away
Thinking was something easy to find again
Only to understand too late
That your love was truly the most they ever had
And that their cowardice would haunt them on

Never underestimate yourself
By the rejection of another
No matter what life throws at you
Your worth only increases
For is in the furnace of suffering
A pure soul is certified with wisdom

Your value is not defined
By what another chooses to think of you
Your value is defined
By what you think of yourself
Think about how you would like to increase
That value you give to yourself

Come to your center and look straight
At the apples of your eyes
Is there anything you want to improve?
Or fix? Or change?
Then do that to be at peace with yourself
But never ever do it
Because of another's misconception of you

Someone who gives no value to your love
Does not deserve your mind space
Someone who does not value your love
Does not deserve your heart's space

Your purified soul can now grow and evolve
To so much better
Look up above to the infinite sky
And see how your dreams can fly
Beyond the clouds

The kind of love you give
Is being searched by many
Be wise next time who you give it to
Stop and think before you again throw your flowers
to the pigs
And wait for your hands to be kissed

Never change the pure nature of your love
Just because a pig didn't get it
Precious Genuine love is not for everyone
But for someone
It means the world

There's no one like you

# Self Love

Self Love
The most important of all the expressions of love
Self-love is usually the most misunderstood
Kind of love
Because it may get mistaken by egoism
Self-love is more
Than merely demanding love for yourself

It is, to be honest, and true to your core
And be happy to be yourself
No matter the circumstances or rejections

To trust in you enough
To prepare to achieve your dreams
And well deserved bright future

It is to think of how amazing you are
To Love yourself before anybody else
To be proud of your stories
And cheer to your achievements

To fill your love cup
Before you connect to other people
When your cup is full
You can rather give than need love from others
Not everyone will give you love
And you won't feel devastated about it
You will be able
To forgive others
And to have compassion

For those who lack Love to give

It is to surround yourself
With an environment that pleases you
To immerse yourself in the harmony
That you can experience
In silence or solitude

It is to treat yourself with respect
And enjoy the connection you share with nature
And the universe

To be kind to yourself
And eat those things you know are good for you
To be aware of your breathing
And take care of your very skin
It is to acknowledge your hurts and failures
And have
An internal healing conversation about them
You then will see
How much peace you can achieve
Within your subconscious mind

It is to find inspiration within your life lessons
There'll always be a good thing to learn
Out of all of them

Your skills to survive a change
Your courage at getting ahead
Despite oppositions

Never let your inner child be neglected
For this

Is the fountain of your youthful approach to life
Self-love is embracing that inner child
While your personal growth forever continues
It is to be grateful for the beautiful memories,
Respectful and compassionate
For the ones that were not
Not anybody's childhood was perfect.
Life throws all types of lessons and trials
To all of us
All is part of what you are made of
And who you are today

With sound self-love, you don't criticize yourself
You observe how you react to different situations
The way you walk, the way you talk
The way you love
To try and educate yourself better

Inner growth never ends
When you love yourself
You are happy to evolve
And nothing will stop you
Every lesson will enhance you
Rather than destroy you
You are your best ally
You are whole and at peace with your inner core

You are one with love
The highest energy in the universe

# Breathe and Relax

Welcome

We all have those moments
When our emotions get the worst of us
Feeling sad, misunderstood, ignored,
Rejected, or exasperated
It is hard to feel calm and at peace

This is a breathing and relaxing exercise
For you to use anytime
Get inside where there is peace, understanding, and
true love
Always available to you

The bell helps you to keep rhythm resonance
Of your breathing and your blood pressure
It is a time for you to ignore
Whatever chaos is outside of you
To stop giving energy and attention to it

To be at one
With your soul

The warmth on your body
Reassuring of your precious life
And all the love
That emanates and goes through you
You are bigger than any problem

Your mind is your garden

Close your eyes and stay in silence here for a few minutes

Before you take any action or make any decision

When the bell stops you can get back to it

But for just a few minutes

Breath

Relax

And Enjoy

# You Are Not Broken

You are not broken.
You are not just your body
In this present moment

You are your mind connected to the infinite
Your soul intertwined with everyone else
Your spirit aligned with that force you call God
You have just awakened to a new chapter
In your physical reality

A chapter where some characters will go
To give space to new ones
A chapter that tests your resilience
As to where you want your story to go

A new way to understand yourself
And what you want in life

Yes, letting go is never easy

Whether you are ready or not
Your story continues
The faster you are aware
You are called by your destiny
The faster you prepare for it
There's nothing you need to fix
It is a process of inner growth
That continues evolving
At your own pace and timing
You will breathe people in and out of your life

There is nothing wrong with that
There's nothing wrong with you

Yes, letting go is never easy
But is exciting when you focus ahead
Being certain that everything
Will get much better

Believe it or not, life is like a stairway
You either continue going up or get back down
When someone tries to bring you down
By breaking up with you
You either let them trip you up
Or continue ahead
Life can be ruthless just like nature
The strong will defeat the weak
Your inner strength is more powerful
Than you think

Your cycle of life continues
Whether someone joins you or not
Evolution won't stop
Your mind won't stop evolving
Unless you keep it paused staring at your past

Life goes on

There is nothing wrong with you
You are not broken
You have feelings
And that is a good sign of humanity
This is just the worst time
To slide down and fall

It is now, a good time for you alone
If you pay good attention
You will learn new things, about yourself and life
Is a good time to take care of yourself
And make yourself
Much more beautiful than before
A time to grow, to learn
And to master your life as you know it

Sooner or later either
That person comes back
Or a much better one comes in
Accepting a breakup
Is not the same as being broken
Accepting a breakup
Is standing firm for you and liberating yourself
From being stuck with someone
Who may have missed seeing the real you
Or never really loved you
Take that break up with both hands
And let it inspire you for the better
To choose better next time
To love yourself even more

You are not broken
A page has turned and
Urge you to renew your truth
Your zest for life
And your true love
For yourself

# Transcend Transmute Transform

Sometimes
A low and narrow passage
Prepares you for something special

Welcome to this visual meditation exercise

Be aware of your breathing

Let yourself be transported
Through the paths of your imagination
And connect
With sensations of what is it that you now want
You are being invited
To be in a progressive state of mind
Within the present moment
Follow your flow of progressive thinking

Leaving old patterns of thought behind
Leaving bad memories behind
Leaving toxic people or anything
That causes you to worry or pain behind
To transcend your situation
As you leave any past painful story behind

To transmute your pain
By brainstorming creative ideas
And required action plan
To transform your thinking pattern
By projecting your dreams for your future
Balance your tri-dimensional focus

Into an infinity of possibilities
Brainstorm new ideas
To update your actual level of knowledge
And wisdom
Ideas that will create new satisfying experiences

Reconnect with your inner self
That inner eye that sees it all
Follow your inner guidance

A new level of commitment to get better
Or to stop bad habits
You will experience new freedom
To enjoy your life's ride
Have fun, be happy
Share it with others

You are not responsible for anyone else's happiness
No one is responsible for yours
It is only a good intention
And the desire of any loving human being

Allow yourself to experience
More safety and security
Abundance, money
And all the pleasures that come with it
Celebrations, Fame, Wealth, Fireworks!
Others are enjoying all this right now
You are welcome to enjoy that too!

You are allowed to have a blast
And to make your dreams come through
To have loads of fun and to enjoy your life

Open the windows of your receptive mind
Where everything and anything is possible
Open your mind to the abundance
In this Universe
An abundance that belongs to you
Allow yourself to

Transcend
Transmute and
Transform

Your story

Your life

# Manifest Your Best You

You are unique
Yet you can express yourself in a myriad of ways
You can vibe so high that toxic people
Can no longer approach you

There are so many new things to learn about
You can turn the page and
Paint a whole different picture of your situation
On any chosen day

Manifest the best you

Do not change your inner essence
Take care of your inner child
But go ahead and improve those areas
That makes you feel insecure in any way
No need to cut your hair but do restyle your look
Buy something new and go about town

Take walks in nature
Listen to inspiring books
Or talks to motivate you
Music that makes you swing
Words that re-assure you

Sit to observe a clear sunset and
Pay attention to the sound of the wind

Manifest the best you

Take a deep breath and be grateful
When you are grateful
Clouds of negativity have to move away

Find an activity or sport that keeps you moving
Dance and sing even if in your shower
Joy will quickly join you

Manifest the best you

Reconnect with loving people in your life
Let go of the toxic ones and
Take your distance

Learn to enjoy being alone and
Enjoy the peace of your own company
Appreciate every single day
You' get better and better

Clear your mind of unwanted thoughts
By replacing them with lighter ones

Adjust your mind just
As an airplane that needs redirection
Every now and then
To get to the desired destination
Depressing thoughts lead you to depression
Appreciation thoughts
Lead you to a happier place
Try meditation and stop your thinking altogether
For a few minutes every day

Manifest the best you

Explore your charm and express your best
You don't harm anyone
By standing for who you are
Those who matter to you
Don't mind
And those who mind
Don't matter to you

Respect others
But never let them
Manipulate you into a people pleaser

You are who you are
Give the best of you

When your happiness is your priority
Happiness is yours

Manifest the best you

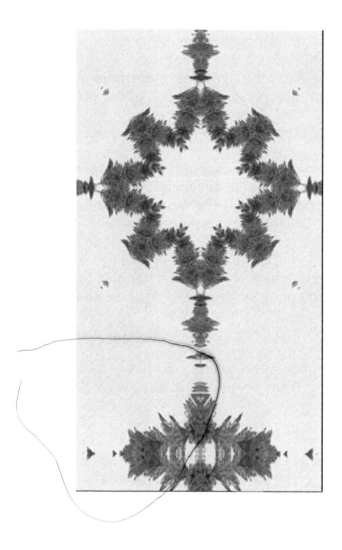

# Reclaim Your Power

Just because someone makes a mistake
Doesn't make him or her toxic
Everyone makes mistakes
And hurt loved ones sometimes
A toxic person is one that hurts you
Over and over again
Convincing you is not a big deal

A toxic person would not apologize for real
They might pretend you did hurt them too
A toxic person is one who never truly understand
How they keep hurting you

As you love this person
You give in to always understanding them
You put your needs and rights second
You forgive
Even when there never was any true apology

This is how you give your power away
What power do you give away?

The power to say no
The power to walk away
The power to be free and love again
The power to ask the universe
For what you deserve
The power to dream big to think big
To expect the best for yourself
The power to command respect and

116

The right to be happy
The power to be truly loved

Reclaim your power
If you want to be happy
You must reclaim this power
You owe it to your constantly hurt self

Reclaim your power
To see people for whom they are
To know what is there for you
To forgive faults
But reject any type of emotional abuse

Reclaim your power
To envision your dream of love
And how you would love to be loved
To believe there is still
Someone better out there for you
To be ready for the abundance of blessings
The universe has in store for you
To understand that you deserve those blessings

Reclaim your power
To see yourself strong and standing firm
When your new life knocks at your door

To feel confident
That you are healed from any pain
That has been on the way to be prepare
To receive true love and peace with open arms

To have so much respect for yourself

Those narcissists cannot shake you up no more
To appreciate what is good in someone
And love the right person deeply

Reclaim your power
To open the doors of your life
Without fear of criticism
To take the reins of your destiny and
Appreciate your life for what it is

To be happy to be alive
Celebrate your health and enjoy
This beautiful and colourful planet
As it has been said before:
To dance as if nobody is watching
And love as if never hurt

Reclaim your power
To deal with your inner struggles to be balanced
As we all do
To find your balance
And know what is best for you

To be concerned with your own
Life and well being
Power to live your life
The best you can

Reclaim your power

# When They Hurt

Toxic people are too complex to analyze
We usually loved them too much
To put such labels on them

Toxic people are usually people
That have been hurt
And never truly healed
If you don't heal your pain
This pain will fester in your heart
And will affect others

You too could become toxic
Toxic people
Are people who live with a buried pain
They are too ashamed to admit
Toxic people don't have the courage
To face the demons
That confronts us at early age
Toxic people are complex to understand

Some toxic people do not love themselves
Enough, if at all
Some never truly forgive
Some always expect the worst
And never truly trust
Some have let their ego run wild
The bigger the ego the deeper the pain
Anyone can become toxic
Me too
You too

We must strive to have a sound mind
And a healthy core

You must acknowledge you're hurt
Your pain, your regrets, and sorrows
You must tell the truth
If only to yourself
Hopefully, you have someone you trust
Or are willing to help you
Don't be afraid to admit to your vulnerability
Let your ego crack
So it won't fool you into hiding the scars

Make sure that pain, hurt, regret or sorrow
Won't fester onto your new life
That your heart is healed
When love calls you again
To clear your mind
And your heart of all resentments

To love your life and yourself
When you love yourself
Then you are able to love others
When they hurt
Is because they have not dealt with
Their own pain or regrets or ego issues

When they hurt you
They also hurt themselves
Be forgiving but move on
Do not accept emotional abuse
Life is not long enough to understand ourselves
And learn from the universe

Let alone to understand others
All we can do is to give them peace

You are free to decide
Whether you can devote your life
To try and help someone
Who won't help themselves
Truth is available to everyone
The Lessons in life are the teachers
To each and every one of us
We all have time to devote to
Our personal inner growth

When they hurt
Do your best to leave them in peace
Help as you can
While you can
And then
Move on

# Heal Your Heart

Welcome, please make yourself comfortable
And watch your breathing
As you synch in and out to the sound and rhythm of
the healing note in the background
This healing note is a timed resonance for you to
follow
The flow of oxygen that fills your lungs
In and out throughout the duration of this self-
introspection
You will increasingly synch easier as you practice
The resonance timing is certified to normalize
Your own heart's assonance
With your breathing and your blood pressure
This introspective meditation brings healing
As it can provide recovery from heartbreak
Pause your thinking at this moment
You are here to take care of yourself

Breathe in

And Breathe out

Let go of your thoughts concerning anything but
your breathing and your heart
Let thoughts float by, without paying any attention
to them, just for now.
There is nothing you need to do right now. Ignore
the outside world
Allow your mind to connect with your core center
Feel what you feel,

If there is fear or sadness there, this is what you
need to face now
Allow you to feel and express any emotions.
If you cry, let the tears flow free and feel yourself
Set the intention to be healed once and for all
Placing one hand on your heart and one hand on the
center of your upper body
Get your mind to be fully present for your heart in
this precious moment.
Continue to breathe focusing on your essence, your
heart, and how you feel.
Take the courage you need to accept what you must
release in order to heal.
You can be totally honest with your own self
You must release your pain from deep within...
You can do that now
With every breath, you will excel the negatives out
from that deep place.
Continue this practice as you breathe at the rhythm
of the healing note.
Allow your mind in revealing the thought or
memory that feeds the pain
Now use your right hand as if pulling a string from
where this awful feeling hides in connection with
that thought
Root out both the thought and pain from where they
connect and hide deep within.
As if you pull the root out of you.
Breath in deep
And Breath OUT

Your heart place has cleared now, and you should feel a sense of relief, if not, repeat this exercise again and even once more until it does.
Your heart will now heal the pure and empty space where that feeling was.
Embrace this as a vision for a moment.
Notice how light you feel
How calm you are feeling now...
Let go of any control.
You don't have to pretend, or do or force anything to happen.
This is all within you and your heart center
You can trust your heart; your heart trusts you
Follow the cool breeze as it flows deep within you
Visualize this breeze as a soft and translucent light flowing through your heart and all your body.
You are now being healed by this light,
You shall no longer be in fear
You may be inspired to love yourself unconditionally even more now
To forgive and move on
You are immersed in your light
You are aware; you are the guard of your heart
You came here to take care of yourself and you have done so.
You have released toxicity and you are clear
This is a very special time
Your heart is breathing new love, your love.

And as you are excited to jump at life again
You allow the cleared space to be open to all the love that life has to offer and the harmony that surrounds you

Let your inner light continue to flow and heal you
Continue to take care of your heart

Continue to take care of yourself.

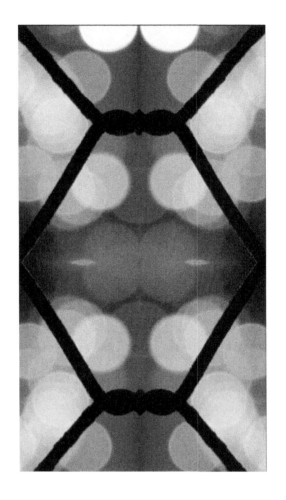

# Closure

The most important step for us to move on
When a chapter ends
Is to find Closure

We linger for the resolution and determination
We need in our minds
Rarely do we get this closure from others
And we must achieve it on our own

Closure is the conviction
That nothing else can be done or said
To reverse the change
When we feel there is something else to do or say
We must achieve that closure

You achieve this closure by stepping back to
Be on observing mode
Looking honestly at yourself and
Realize you must take some time to grieve

To be kind to yourself and acknowledge you already
did all you could do
To forgive others and understand
They have given what they could
You will then stop asking an apple tree
To give you oranges

Closure enables you to redesign your hopes and
Plans for your future
To look at the past with gratitude

Because every experience shape your character

We are all complex personalities
That can emotionally merge only for a time
When differences arrive
We disconnect from those
Who no longer match with us
In order to reconnect to others
Who will do in time
If you lower your vibration
You may attract the same type or much worse
If you make progress, they will be better for you
When that happens
The same applies
To those who disconnect from us

We have been programmed to believe romantic love
should last forever
And ideally, it should do
But not until we mature
To be in a solid place of understanding
This of course has nothing to do with age
When both people click and match at that place
Forever can be achieved

We must accept that changes
Within our relationships
Will happen
As we grow and evolve
We must still believe
There are infinity of opportunities
To achieve our dreams
Whether that forever means

Joining someone else
Or not

We must get exes off pedestals and recognize
They don't belong in those dreams
Whatever qualities they had
That hook your idealistic thoughts on
Can be found in someone new
It may take some time for a new person to arrive but
sooner or later it will happen

You can use this time
To be in a much better place
So you can match with someone of a kind

If for whatever reason you may remain alone
Your self-love, peace, and freedom
Are meant to fulfil you
To celebrate your life
And either way, you can achieve happiness
It is best to be your own honest happy self
Than sacrificing your inner being
For someone else's ideal
Take anyone you may have placed on a pedestal and
set your vision for yourself instead

Forgiveness and Gratitude are the keys
To opening the gates to a renewed mind
A renewed mind will produce a higher vibration
To attract better people in your life

When you can accept the change and
Be able to forgive others and yourself

You find the Closure you need to truly Move On

Closure is done
When you can come to terms with the past and
Can stop trying to fix it
You look ahead to your future instead and
Start working on yourself and your dreams

You don't hide
You are not angry
You may be sad but not devastated
You simple "Be"

You are open to the unfolding of your story
Trusting the many ways the universe
Can bring you more good
Than you can imagine right now

When you achieve closure
You are free to start a new chapter
You are ready to begin
Anew

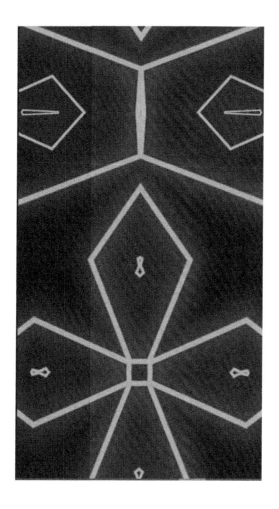

# Not a Problem but an Opportunity

A breakup is not a problem
It is an opportunity
An opportunity to open your eye
And face what is true
To reassess yourself, your life

And opportunity to take time to understand
Actions and reactions

An opportunity to learn new things
To improve your life
In many little ways
Or in a big way
An opportunity to create
Or do something differently

Look yourself in the mirror and
Accept yourself completely
If there is something you don't like
Look for ways to change it
Improve it
Or learn to love it the way it is
You cannot block your happiness because of it
Any longer
Look around you and do the same for the place you
live or work

Watch what you eat, what you drink
What you watch and listen to
As this is what you nourish

Your body and your mind with
Everything that comes into your system
Recreates you

When you get through the stages of a breakup
When you accept the imminent change
You will find powerful opportunities to
Transform your life

While you disappear of sight
From people who may be draining your energy
You have the opportunity to transform and
Redesign your future

A breakup is not a problem but an opportunity
An opportunity for you and the other person
To reassess your love
Either you will become stronger
Or better choices sooner or later appear

Through this time, the best you can do
Is to improve your self
You have this time to brainstorm ideas
That will benefit your life in many ways
Give space to others to prove themselves right
Give others the benefit of missing you

Wake up and smell the flowers
The earth has not stopped spinning in orbit
Time waits for no one
It is an opportunity to be alone and
Give ourselves "Me" time
To evaluate and love yourself and

Your life much more

To understand human nature and
Grow to forgive others
To cheer yourself up and recognize
Your strengths and qualities

To value yourself and protect your heart

There are 7 billion people
Sharing life on this planet
Breaking up with that one person
Is not a problem to be fixed
It is an opportunity
For you
To bloom
Anew

# Expect the Unexpected

A new beginning challenges your faith
You don't really know what to expect

We create our destiny as we walk on
Faith is taking hold of dreams coming through

We don't need to be certain
We don't have to feel secure
We just trust that love is in charge
And continue to walk on

We don't have to prove anything to anyone
We must be humble and start from where we are
We just have to be true to ourselves
When you let go and let love in
The Universe takes charge
You allow the flow of its energy
To push you through

We are all called to get lessons from love
You meet people who
Get the best and worse out of you
You get to know yourself and others better

Know what you need to change
Know what you can improve
Know what you must stand for
Know what you should strive for
Know what you must give up
Know what you should never change

You are the one who reassesses yourself
At every turn of every page in your book

Expect the unexpected and be prepared
If things don't go to plan
Expect opposition when your dreams are big
Expect to be uncomfortable
When you desire to change
Expect you cannot control anything
Expect to give your best and sometimes
Get nothing back
Expect conflict when all you want is peace
Expect the unexpected and prepare yourself
To trust

A new beginning starts with a setback
Just like the arrow is pulled back
Before is shut forward
Change arrives all of a sudden and
This is the first sign
When you are experiencing a setback
Use this time to prepare
As you'll go forward at a higher speed
When your time is due

You are that arrow
In the hands of the universe
Aimed to the moon
You might hit the stars

Expect the Unexpected and
Prepare yourself

For the best future vision, you can dream of
Prepare yourself
For happiness against all odds
Prepare yourself
To trust
When you cannot see what the future holds

Prepare yourself
To laugh, to dance, to be happy
Prepare yourself to be loved
Prepare yourself to love

Expect the Unexpected

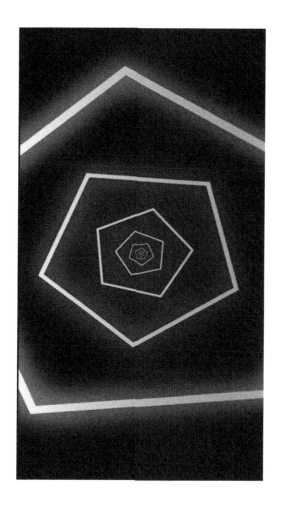

# Hypnotic

Welcome

This hypnotic exercise will help you to de-clutter your negative thought pattern and get you into a positive and supportive frame of mind for self-confidence and success.
Get yourself comfortable and relax into the affirmations trance whether your naked ear understands them or not, your subconscious mind will absorb them. Rest assured all affirmations are beneficial for you to replace self-sabotage thoughts with empowered ones.

You are willing to connect with infinite intelligence
That inner wisdom that knows the answers to your deeper questions
That inner world where you find solutions to all of your conflicts

You have full support for your dreams
Your universe desires your happiness
You have a unique and valuable story in you, you forgive past hurts.
You are excited about a loving and successful future

All that has happened makes you who you are, strong and wise
You have learned your lessons, you are constantly evolving

You understand who you are and what you want

You understand where you are and what you can improve
You forgive and forget what you must
You deserve to see yourself enjoying your life much more

You are a beautiful person inside and out
You now express yourself better
You take responsibility for your actions
You allow yourself to shine
You allow your charm to show
You see any challenge as an opportunity to shine through

You are strong to face and follow your truth
You are magnanimous yet humble; you have compassion for yourself and others
You are wise and balanced

You are successful in all your efforts
You attract lovely people into your life
You are grateful you are alive. You love your life
Every new day is an opportunity to be better
Every day you get better and better

You surround yourself with positive and lovely people
You attract abundance and money flows to you easily
You live with joy and peace
You are ready for more progress and success
You are guided to be at the right place at the right time

You inspire respect, you respect others and yourself
You deserve to be happy and so you are

Smile, you are a wonderful human being.

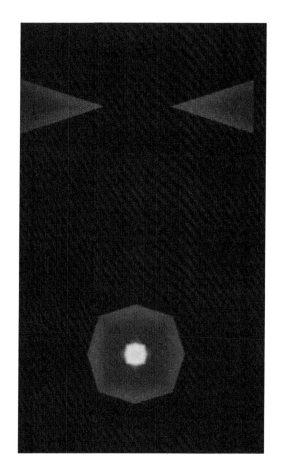

# Detach and Let Go

You may have loved them
Way longer than you should
You may feel they were everything you wanted
Yes, they were....not anymore

One of the saddest truths
We must come to accept
Is that the person you thought
Was the perfect match for you
Is no longer the same
Some fundamentals have changed and
That person you loved lives only in the past

It is one of the hardest realizations
But one that gives us the strength to let go
You have also changed
You no longer match
Is not the love you now want

Change is movement
Change is learning new ways to be and to love
Once your lessons have been learned
You are due to upgrade
Either together or go on separate ways

The person who leaves first
Is not always in a better position
In their game called "love"
If they betrayed true love
Or left without a valid reason

They are due for a new lesson
Don't let appearances fool you
Sometimes, it requires the universe
To teach them some other lessons
For them to realize
What they had while they took it for granted
If you believe in karma
You know that no one gets away from it

That person has decided
To follow new energy in them
They are no longer
The person you were in love with
Sadly, the person you could trust and laugh with
Is not there anymore in the same way
They changed
They chose another path
A path you belong no more

It is hard...

It feels as if that person died
And someone new took over
That part of them has died
The part that you loved
The part that loved you

Trust all happens for a reason
Grieve for a time
Then embrace new energy too.
Transmute your frustration and pain
Into creating a vision for your desires

If you are one faithful to true love and your thoughts
are pure
Love keeps alive in you and blooms all over again I
In everything you are passionate about
Trust the process. Take care of yourself
Focus your passion and
Strive for your best-ever self
Stay still before your past and know there's nothing
else you must do
Go with the flow
You are not alone

Is time to appreciate and
Cheer your other types of love
Family love, nature love, spiritual love
Continue to fall in love with your own life
Believe in your future

Don't be afraid of change
Stop mourning the past and
Welcome the birth of a new beginning
Soon you will understand
Your situation and yourself better
Soon you will realize that person in the past
Would not fulfil who you have become
You are due for an upgrade in love
And what you thought was a loss
Has guided you to your very best
Trust the process
Detach and Let go

# Don't Give Up

Don't let appearances fool you
You can win at every step, you are powerful
You conquer your battles
As you keep your smile on
Be happy with yourself
Do what you love
Go wherever you want to go
Don't give up

Don't give up being your genuine self
Don't give up trusting Love
Don't give up enjoying the simple things in life
Don't give up dreaming of better things to come

Live to love who you are
Don't give up on you
When a door closes, another one opens up
Somewhere else

Stop swimming against the current
Learn to follow your inner guidance
There is a new flow to follow

Don't give up on what you want
Make a turn when time is up
Changing direction is not giving up
Is to strive forward going with a new flow

Don't give up your inner child
Don't give up your mature mind

Don't give up the perfect blending of contrasts
That makes you unique
Don't give up improving yourself
To find your best

Don't give up your inner wisdom
Don't give up having fun
All experiences keep you evolving and growing
Don't give up your essence, your loving nature
Don't give up your innocence, your humility
Don't give up your kindness

Don't give up on your dreams
Don't give up feeling complete and enough
Don't give up your search
For all the other things you want
Don't give up believing in your future
Don't give up gratitude

Stand for your truth, strive for your ideals
Try to understand your and others human nature

Don't give up on love

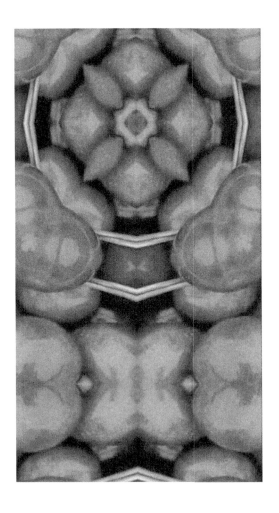

# Love

Love is in you
To be able to love others you must love
Yourself first
The cup in your heart is full
Before you fill another's
True Pure Love will never fail
Love has always taken care of you

Love was there when you were born
Love has been beating within your heart all along
Love made every inch of your bones grow
Love is here with you

Love has been with you all the way
Love was there when you learned to walk
Love has seen you fall
Love has protected you from sudden death
Love is keeping you alive

Loving others is a challenge
Sometimes we hurt each other
As we learn our lessons
Love is not to be blamed for failures
Love intentions are forever pure

Love is sharing all we are
Mix and match
Sometimes hurts
Love will forever be love
The most powerful energy in this universe

Love rules above all odds

Love is not followed by everyone
But love is in everyone anyway
Some hide from it
Some lie to it
Some deny it
Is up to them
Love is everyone's best

Connecting to your truth leads you to your love
Love is there when no one is around
Love is there when you reflect on your actions
Love is there
To give you honest answers

Love is ready to shine through to you
Love is there when you learn your lessons
Love supports you when you fall
Love has never let you down
Expand your mind to see where love is

Love is in you
You are in love

# Access to Full Video Chapters

Searching the following Link:

https://youtube.com/playlist?list=PLyGmV2_9TK8z-w-ryvw8Z7o3b5fohMEbA

**YouTube@Sense4Love**

*You are never alone*

*We are all learning together...*

*Wishing this book and video system*

*Wakes up the greatest love for yourself*

*Your life*

*Gloria Betancur*

Printed in Great Britain
by Amazon

23276186R00091